Illuminate My Way

Illuminate My Way

A collection of Poems
by Clare M Ashton

THE CHOIR PRESS

First published in 2006 by The Choir Press

Copyright © Clare M. Ashton

The right of Clare Ashton to be identified as the author of this work has been asserted in accordance with the Copyright, Designs and Patents Act 1988.

All rights reserved. No part of this publication may be reproduced or transmitted in any form or by any means, electronic or mechanical including photocopying, recording or any information storage or retrieval system, without prior permission in writing from the publisher.

ISBN-10: 0-9535913-5-2
ISBN-13: 978-0-9535913-5-0

Produced by Action Publishing Technology Ltd, Gloucester
www.actiontechnology.co.uk

Contents

7th July 2005	1
Abandoned	3
Almighty King	4
Alpha and Omega	5
Angel Voices	7
Babylon	9
Boat Ashore	11
Boat of Peace	13
Bow of Peace	15
Bread and Fishes	17
Bread Broken	18
Brightened Flame	19
Broken Hearts, Haunted Eyes	20
Building The Temple	21
Calvary Calling	22
Calvary's Journey	25
Cascading Crown	28
Chains and Freedom	28
Changing Seasons	32
Christ	34
Christmas in a Box	35
Cleansing Flame	36
Come Almighty	38
Come, Dance	39
Dance in the darkness	40
Dance of Victory	42
Dare You?	44
Dawn of Victory	46
Enthralling	48
Epiphany	49

Evening Prayer	50
Flowers Unchained	51
Fury Untamed	53
Glowing Embers	55
God of Compassion	58
God of Our Salvation	59
Headlong Into Your Arms	62
Heartbeat of Peace	64
Innocent Child	66
Just Surrender	68
Kyrie Eleison	70
Labouring One	71
Liberation Day	72
Life's Journey	74
Light the Fire	75
Little Child	75
Maybe Then....	79
Mighty One	81
Merciful Father	84
My God	85
Nowhere To Run	87
Oasis	88
Old Armour	90
Open Our Hearts – Pentecost	92
Our Father	93
Pacesetting	94
Papa	96
Peace Unbidden	97
Pictures of Faith	99
Rage and peace	102
Rain and Drought	104
Raindance	106
Reach Out	108
Redemption	109
Remembrance	112
Rest	113
Rivers and Greed	114
Saviour in the Mirror	117
Scars of Beauty	118

Selfish Steward	120
Shalom	122
Sometimes	123
Space	125
Spirit A-Sighing	129
Spirit of Peace	131
Starry Night	132
Stormy Waters	133
Surrounded	134
Take the Time	136
Teetering Temptation	138
Tossed Leaves	140
The Barriers	142
The Carpenter's Son	143
The Cloister	144
The Kingdom of the Poor	145
The Leaf	147
The Sacred Lonely Olive Tree	148
The Shelter	150
Thorns of Pain	153
Throne of Grace	155
Travelling Home	157
Under the Tree	159
Waves of Love	161
When You Listen	162
Wolves of the Heart	164
Yearning	166
120 Seconds	167

'To all my spiritual companions who have shared my journey'

7th July 2005

Flowers mean beauty
This one, rage,
Proudly, brutally, flowered on the world's stage

People
Their lives shattered
Suddenly all that mattered
Was life.

Frantically, they race
Fighting to retrace
Steps back to life
And the light

Once more the door has opened
Evil crept in
Once more
We begin to heal

The wounds
The scars
One not seen
Still mars,
Confidence shaken
Nerves taken

Yet we know
In the kindness people show
The pain will grow

Less each day

For those taken from us
Snatched away
All we can do is pray and say

Hold them to your heart Lord
And heal our wounded cry
They snatched away our loved ones
In anger we ask why

We'll never know the answers
Why fate took them that day
Why men with anger filled hearts
Snatched random lives that day

So heal the broken heart Lord
And soothe their aching soul
Of shattered lives be a part Lord
Lead them to the path
That makes them whole
And leads them to

Your peace

Abandoned

Abandoned, I hear the waves crashing
Abandoning themselves
To the mercy of the cliffs
That protected me
As I too surrender

Salt fills the air
Assails my senses
I rise
Lean against rocks
Gazing at the waves
Restful now

Their peace calls to me
And yet I hear another voice
Lapping in their peaceful caress

The shore embraces the waves
Calling them home
I too am called to the peace
Beyond the world's imagining
Far above our broken understanding

Come, my child, rest awhile
Take the chance to dance in the waves
That greet the shore, to once more

Be free

Almighty King

This is your God, this is your king
He loves us so, and will his joy bring

Here is your God, and here is our redeemer
Yes, here is our God
And here is our love deep inside, that keeps us whole

Deepest mystery, our God has set us free
He loves us, so you see
That he sent his son, His only Son
To die in pain on Calvary

So when you see the world made by my own hand
Look at the oceans, see the land
And feel the power of my love

Yes I stride the world, scatter the stars from my hands
The mountains are my foothills, and my love pours over many lands
Yes my love pours over many lands

And when the world makes you feel small
Remember still my peaceful call
Turn your ear once more to me
And I will set your Spirit free
To soar

Alpha and Omega

He flung the stars into space, He climbs the
highest mountains
Striding forth in our universe, and this is our
God

The one in whom creation finds its true beginning
The voice of the world at peace
There when each day is dawning
Crying for each child's release

Yes, this is the Father, this is our friend
The mighty one, who created our world
He longs to reach out to all, and give us peace

This is indeed our God
The one whom the waves and land adore
Yes, and when he sees our world
Battered by pettiness and wars
He weeps once again to see
The damage done to you and me

For this God may well be awesome
But this Father is a friend
And He is walking beside us
From journey's start to its end

The one who flings the stars, and sets them in
the sky
Would like nothing better than to sing His child
a lullaby

So hush, this world, so weary and tired
He will help you to once more be inspired
And release you from the pain and give you
peace
From the world, he can release
The chains that bind us so

And when you feel you can't go on
And all the hope you feel is gone
Climb into His arms and let it go
He will tell you, if you don't already know

How He loves you

Angel Voices

Can you hear them? Angel voices
Break the silence as heaven rejoices

For the night when heaven meets earth
And angels herald the Saviour's birth

So hurry on, fly through the fields
As heaven to earth, it's treasure yields

And gaze with awe, and wonder rare
At humble manger, in stable there

With ox and ass, and shepherd too
Many will pass, be born anew

Some days later, the kings appear
Offering homage, they draw near

Bring forth their gifts
Gold, frankincense and myrrh
They leave their homage
And worship there

The Son of God, the Son of Man
Who mountains trod, when time began

The newborn babe starts to cry
And is soothed with Mary's lullaby

This little child will mankind save
With His victory over the grave

So hush my child and go to sleep
The ox and ass their vigil keep

We gaze in wonder while we may
The Servant King asleep in the hay

And as He enjoys sleep's gentle release
Let us adore the prince of Peace

Babylon

Babylon, the bullets flying
Babylon, the men are dying
Babylon, the women crying
And your children sighing

Once again blood lines your streets
And once more, doomed to repeat
History ancient in days new
When bloodshed soaks your roads anew

And the people once again
Tire of counting the loss of men
Lost in yet another attack
Is this what happened to their Iraq?

Is this what happened, hear their cries
As bombs play their lullabies
And soothe to sleep their young men
Never will they awake again

For their sleep is that of death
And with every laboured breath
Their lifeblood seeps away
Is this the price we have to pay?

When those who help are taken away
And locked far from the light of day
When people who will give their time
Are prisoners in this crazy mime

Where is the reason, where is the sense?
For keeping with this vain pretence?
Carers slaughtered, all in vain
And blood once more will fall like rain

You lost your soldiers oft time that's true
For reasons old and reasons new
But young men lost in this war's toil
Are sacrificed for cheaper oil.

The sword is blood stained once again
With the stain of your young men
The flower of your nation's youth
Should be told a simple truth

The war that's waged will see no end
Enemy or chosen friend
For Muslim, Christian, Gentile, Jew
This war is old, yet ever new

It's time to hand those weapons down
It's time your face forgot its frown
It's time this war should reach its end
And enemies call each other friend

Maybe, just maybe, we will find
We change our heart, we'll change our mind
And the last bomb be the last attack
In this wounded land, your Iraq

Boat Ashore

When the world seems a hostile place
I once more gaze upon your face
And somehow life makes sense
Once more

And as the world retreats
I sit at your feet
And their words don't matter
Any more

For somehow when I'm here
The world can disappear
And I won't mind

For their world is not my world
Their banner unfurled
Is not my cause
And the wars they wage
Cause only pain and grief

And so I stand
With Your sword in my hand
Knowing your word
Is my one true shield
I will not yield
To their petty war

So I will stay and will pray
That in Your way
Safe from pain
I will remain

I clamber inside, the boat I guide
And deep inside You are my guide
My compass points, direction true
And redirects my soul to You

So as I gaze to future days
The world doesn't seem
Quite so large a place

For when I see men engulfing me
I turn to the tree
And once more gaze at your face

For you are my God, I trust in You

Boat of Peace

Here is your saviour
your Lord and your God
For you are walking
where saints and angels trod

Here is our saviour and here is our king
Merciful Saviour your praises we sing
For your love spans our world
And the power of your love sets us on fire

To sing of your love
The love that sets us free
And gives us peace
Joy and lasting dignity

It gives us worth and gives us love
And heals our deepest fear
Wiping away with the wounds in his hand
The pain and every tear

I could love you for ever
And still never love you enough
My all belongs to you
My Father of love

I will cross that river
When I am talking to you
Somehow that river
Isn't deep when I'm with you

And the boat beckons me on
To healing and peace
The release I yearn for
Is in Your eyes
And in your voice
As I reach for you, Brother and friend

Bow of Peace

There are times I understand
As you reach out for my hand
That the longed for Promised Land
Is but a breath away

And I see those children cry
For the rainbow in the sky
Shows me once again
How you made that vow to men
How we forgot

The colours with their glowing hue
Remind us all anew
Of old Noah and his ark
And how tending that spark, we all were saved

How easily it seems, we get lost in dreams
And blinded lose our way
From your glorious day, into broody silence

When my pleas for love are heard
You reach down, and without a word
Turn your ear to broken child
Whose heart so meek, so mild, is torn

Show the lost ones gone astray
That you, the Light, the Truth the Way
Are ready with your arms
Outstretched, the world's charms
Cannot offer the peace
And the release Your love alone can give

And once we turn our heads away
From night's distraction to day
We will once more see the way, to live

And that rainbow in the sky
Will once again make spirits fly
As children of God once again
Turn away from angry men
And live in peace

Bread and Fishes

I want to talk with you, I long to walk with you
Help me to make it through, as darkness surrounds me

And when the daylight dawns,
stunned by each new morn
I feel the sunlight, warm, and your love astounds me

It takes my breath away, all that I want to say
Vanishes with the day, for your love surrounds me

As I see bread and fish, and sit by the shore
To eat such a simple dish, and know peace once more

As your love surrounds me, I see in the day
Peace and love that ground me, I can't go astray

So I will remain here, Take space and take time
Away from my old fear, and claim love that's mine

Refreshed, I will wander, no more lost I see
For your love is present, and it surrounds me

Bread Broken

Bread that is broken will set us all free
And the wine, it is poured
By the One from Galilee

Do this, He told us, in remembrance of me
I release all your bondage from Calvary's tree

And as I give freely, a life to you all
I ask that you only pay heed to my call

The call that I echo from the poor and the weak
The ones with no refuge and no chance to speak

For whenever you care for the least of my kin
You care for My Spirit implanted within

For My Spirit lies deep down in each person's heart
And within their soul a fire will start

A fire that burns brightly and will not fade away
Whether trials and troubles appear on their way

So, as we watch closely and He washes our feet
Please bear in mind, brethren, we will take and eat

And the bread that is broken, the wine that is poured
Will lead us in prayer, to Christ Jesus, the Lord

Brightened Flame

The flame burns bright, the night flees
Dawn creeps in, and the touch of the Father's hand
Once more
Draws back the veil of anguish
Seen in the doors to the soul
Broken, not whole

Wounded children
Once more resting
In peace
In You

Broken Hearts, Haunted Eyes

See in broken hearts and haunted eyes
In wounded souls, heart rending sighs
Echo still those anguished cries
First heard on Calvary

And yet, those words can once again
Heal the pain of wounded men
And now the prisoner can be free
For the Risen One brings dignity

And no more will men in fear
Quake as darkness ever near
Will quench the flickering, wavering flame
Made strong in the power of His Name

So once more, we will see
Gazing once more past Calvary's tree
The power for greater than the grave
Through which the power of God can save

O Spirit of God, please whisper to me
As I stand before Calvary's tree
Show me dear Father, once again
The wounded child in the hearts of men

Building The Temple

The bricks go down slowly, hot baked in the sun
The toil of the labourer showing work has begun
The heat from the day makes us hungry and tired
  The work undertaken has been God-inspired

As the days and the nights follow on in our lives
  And each of our souls, for the Gospel strives
    The temple of God, built within our hearts
The kingdom of God on this earth we did start

As the bricks of the Gospel are laid in the world
And the banners of love are so boldly unfurled
The love that we spread causes ripples to spread
And new life to blossom from the spiritually dead

We're building the temple, come build it with me
    And labour with love and with dignity
    Giving Our Saviour a place He can dwell
In the place that you and I and He know so well

Yes, build Him a temple, right here in your heart
  And let now the Gospel, in it's fullness start
To break down the shackles, to set your soul free
    And proclaim the year of our own liberty

    The job is ongoing, the labourers few
  The Kingdom of God has a place just for you
So take up the shovel, the pick and the hod
  Together we'll build this temple for God

Calvary Calling

Was it you that spoke to me
Or merely wind sighing in a tree?
Was it you that called my name
Trying my wild heart to tame

Was it you that led the way
When paths could lead me astray
Kept me safe and kept me warm
Away from danger and from harm

Did I see you when I fell?
And heard the words that hurt so well
Was it you that picked me up
And stayed by me when things got rough

It's easy to stay when weather fair
Warms the skin and ruffles hair
Not so easy I know well
When weather turns to ill, and hell

When fear comes knocking at the door
And faced with deep emotion raw
The storms inside rage far and wide
And it's not safe to even hide

Was it you that lit the fire
That gives the word that will inspire
The fear that so long held sway
To yield to peace at break of day

And when at last one day I stand
With sun in hair and warmth on hand
The storms that raged still make their mark
But the fire of peace has lit a spark

So give me strength and help me stand
With peace upon a distant land
The old fears and pain long since lost sway
As night once more gives in to day

And if the words I hear are true
All you ask for me to do
Is help the others who are there
And reach out to them in their despair

For long ago, I felt, I know
The surest way to help me grow
Was someone who was just like me
To help me on the road to Calvary

So, as I gaze at the lonely hill
And hear the silence echo still
With one, single, piercing cry
It sounds like a battle cry

Come walk with me, and wake once more
The peace and joy that destroys war
For there is none, save you and me
That can set these prisoners free

And if you look, and if you dare
You see inside you love to share
And see the Christ in all their eyes
The ones the world says you should despise

And see instead of angry men
The ones who would begin again
For these He died, He held the key
And broke the chains, on Calvary

Calvary's Journey

Can I say? How my heart is bursting
Can I tell you? My soul is thirsting
With a thirst no one else can satisfy

I saw you
The cross upon your shoulder
The crowd, raucous, noisy
Fear almost tangible
As they mock your progress

The streets are narrow
Their faces crowd you in
Fear and rage etch their way
Into their lives, yet you begin

They blindly follow
Their salvation so near
Yet they cannot see
And cannot feel
The words that you can hear

"Father, the cup you have for me
Will set your children free
Yet the taste, bitter in my mouth
Speaks of sacrifice to me"

"Give me the strength
As I climb Calvary's hill
To love the ones I now see
Who howl against your will"

Their fear blinds their heart
The heart that could betray
The fact that they are thirsting too
And so they turn away

But the well is deep, the well is rich
The love is ever there
And the longest desert has oases
The hope follows despair

And as the tomb is laid asunder
And the Lord of life is there
The fear that etched the faces Lord
Has fled, there's no anguish, and no care

The Lord of life has conquered
For all time death and sin
So when your heart is thirsting
Let the well of love begin

To fill your heart with its peace
It's strength and courage too
So that my child you will be blessed
In all you say and do

And when the well seems dry, child
As often times it will
Release the noise around you
And once more, child, be still
Take the time, once again
Drink deeply from the well
And once again, as oft before
We'll listen and we'll tell

Of water that will satisfy
And tell us we can dare
While others did Him crucify
He will once more share

His peace

Cascading Crown

The water cascading peacefully down
Reminds me of a thorny crown
Shows me again a pierced side
Wherein a broken child can hide

And deep inside the peaceful cave
My heart has chance once more to rave
The anger deep inside of me
Can be expressed, can set me free

For safe within this cave of mine
I sense a peace and love divine
Who judgest not, does not condemn
And gives me space from angry men

Who gives me time to ease my fears
And lick my wounds, and shed the tears
Who if expressed any other way
Would never see the light of day

So I will let my spirit free
And let it breathe in liberty
So I can venture once again
Into a world of broken men

Sure in the knowledge, deep inside
My heart has somewhere safe to hide
And when I hear that broken call
I run and find my waterfall

And peace

Chains and Freedom

Here is love beyond all measure
Here is peace and joy beyond compare
Will you stand always at the water's edge?
Or come join with me, live and dare?

Will you be bound by the things you see?
Or climb in the boat and follow me?
Will you leave fear behind?
The rage of mankind
Will you at last be at liberty?

For the world will take your heart and bind your soul
It will rage and take your chance to be whole
Walk again along the river
Don't be captured by the shore
Longing to be with me,
Human and so much more

Take the oars and row out deep
Past where all your fears sleep
I will take you far away
To the dawn of a new day

Here I hold liberty
In my wounded feet, hands and side
Climb into my wounds
From the world hide

Your heart is wounded and sore
I have felt it and so much more
There is nowhere safer to be
Than deep inside of me

And when I feel your heart beating
In perfect time
The love will be repeating
In your heart and mine

The world is aching too
Despite the pain it pours onto you
I will ask you to
Help me heal our world

For every child that comes to me
There are more in agony
Pain has ensnared them
As it did you

So as you stand in fear
Yours aren't the only tears
To be shed in pain
Confusion and fear

I only ask my child
That your heart, so mild
Will listen to my call
When I want you to hear

And much as it pains you so
I would like you to go
Witness to my love
Tell I am so near

For Father to all am I
I sing a lullaby
My Son I sent to die
That all may be free

And when you hear the call
My Holy Spirit falls
And no more the chains will bind
For you will be free

Changing Seasons

Mighty branches, climbing boldly
Sentinels stretching towards the sky
Strain to hear a gentle whisper
Floating on the autumn sky

Reminisces of the spring
Float unbidden slowly by
The summer gone, the winter enters
Her beauty heard in the wind's cry

Ice dancing in her blue eyes
Snow falling softly among her tresses
Sleet and rain her escort comprise
Maidens in beauteous dresses

Melodies weave gently through the autumn mist
Graceful, eloquent songs of peace
Telling the ones open to listen
Of winter's gentle release

Winter merely minds the new life
Carefully hidden beneath the ground
Far beyond the frost's strife
Prepared for spring's first sound

Look beyond the sentinel trees
Beyond the floating autumn mist
Open your heart to the winter's peace
And let your soul's worries cease

Autumn, winter, summer and spring
The Master tends them all in turn
Listen to His children sing
As deep within His Spirit burns

So take heart in the season's change
Look beyond the autumn tree
The beauty, so stark and strange
Points to Christ's victory

Sin and death stand with no power
As the tree of Christ paid our price
The death and rising, His finest hour
The blameless one, perfect sacrifice.

Seasons all, ever changing
Life and love cycle once more
Death has lost the final sting
For Christ the Lord unlocked the door

And as we gather with the saved ones
Hell's gates yield their key
God's warriors march on proudly
Secure in His victory

So, watch the seasons as they cycle
Secure in the Saviour's love
And wait with longing ever deepened
For the call to God above

Christ

Christ, he lives in you, Christ, he lives in me
Lord, we know it's true, so come and set us free

Christ, He feels our pain, He senses all our fear
Beside you, He'll remain, always staying near

And when the rain is falling, blue skies are far away
You'll hear Him gently calling, Showing you the way

Christ, babe in the manger lives in you and me
In the eyes of a stranger, pleading poverty

Reach out to them today, over this Christmastide
Yes, reach out to Christ today, in His wounds you can hide

Christmas in a Box

Christmas is stored in a box,
Taken out for the world to see
People crowded around the Christmas tree
Little children, faces alight with glee

All the boxes are opened wide
Except for a small one deep inside
One child alone, lost, afraid
Walks to the tree and sees laid

One small parcel left alone
Thinks we are both the same, both alone
They take a chance, reach with shaking hands
Not making a noise, no demands

With fearful hands the package is ripped
The ribbon cut, the paper stripped
What is inside, can you see?
The one package left under the tree

Stars in the sky, babe in the manger
Reaching out both to friend and stranger
Take hold of fear, let go of pride
Open the box and peer inside

Yes when you are weary,
And you've taken your knocks
It is time to take Christmas
Out from the box

Cleansing Flame

Lord the flame burns so bright
In the shadow of deepest night
Let it burn again
Burn again
In the hearts of the broken one
Make undone
The pain that is borne

Take the hurt away, lead them to the day
Lord take away deepest fear
Show us you are ever near

Soothe our pain away, and into the new day
We will emerge in your peace
With a love that will never cease

Wash us once more Lord, You are our lasting reward
Cleanse our sins away,
And the new day will dawn

Once more we will see
The love that sets us free
From every tear
When you are near
Your presence is here
Guarding our hearts
From all that will wound
All that will wound our broken hearts

Gaze once more at your child
We are again undefiled
Wash our pain away
In your love let us stay

Come Almighty

Come Almighty to deliver
Grant your wounded children peace
Come, ever graceful giver
From our constant wars, us release

Let your justice like a river
Flow over our barren hearts
For like a mighty river
As a tiny trickle starts

Your love cascades over mountains
Fear and loneliness swept away
Peace and justice flow like fountains
As your light shows the way

And once more we can see
As we lay down our sword and shield
That war is no answer Lord
To your love, our weary hearts yield.

Come, Dance

Come, dance in the sunshine
Come laugh in the rain
Come, feel my peace touch you
In my love remain

Come, dance in the river
And fly to the sea
Feel once more healing
As you are set free

Free to be loving
Free once more to give
For when you are loving
Then you truly start to live

And reach to those who cannot see
And those who cannot dance
He who hangs on Calvary's tree
Gave all children the chance

To dance in the river, to laugh in the rain
To float in His ocean, free from old pain

Let go as He heals you, let go and be free
Let go and relish His true liberty

Dance in the darkness

Could you dance in the darkness as you
dance in the light
When the world in its starkness turns
from day into night

Can you live with the sorrow and endure
all the pain
Knowing full well tomorrow
The sun will then reign

Can you reach to the lonely
Can you feel their despair
Can you be with them only
To show that He cares?

Will you walk with the wounded
Will you dance with the lame
Will you tell all around you
Of the joy of His Name?

Can you listen to cries
From the heart that is broken
Discounting the lies
That Satan has spoken?

Dare you reach for the sunlight
Dare you fly to the stars?
Can you see in the moonlight
The marks of His scars

Scars of love borne so proudly
In the depth of the night
Shouting boldly and loudly
The result of the fight

The end of the battle
With sorrow and fear
Shows when the night is fading
That the day is now here

Take the hand that is riven
With the nails of the world
Take the love that is given
When the banner's unfurled

And the man who has loved us and set
us all free
Will join us again in the dance of victory

Dance of Victory

I dance in the sunshine, and I dance in the rain
I'm there in the laughter, and I'm there in the pain

I'm the sweet sense of wonderment, no cares
can destroy
And the love almost tangible in each girl and boy

I walk in the shadows and I walk in the light
I'm there in the deepest fear that stalks in the night
I'm comfort and laughter when the love is so far
And I touch all the wounds, and heal every scar

I reach out to comfort all the ones in despair
I touch them, revealing that My love is still there
My love burns out brightly like a strong shining flame
And I draw all men to me, giving praise to My Name

As I raise on my cross, lifted high for all to see
The strength of my witness, on my Calvary
Showing death has no power now my Father does reign
Spells the end of the prison of sorrow and pain

When the shackles of fear bite deep in your soul
And the anguish inside makes you feel so old
The key of your freedom is the cross of His pain
The lock is unbolted the day you let Him reign

The streets are much brighter than your
dungeon of fear
The joy and rejoicing once His Spirit is near
The dawn of the life in you, so long locked away
Gives a strength once again to face a new day

Join with me and we will once more dance
Rejoice in the fact we are given the chance
To set the downtrodden and the prisoner free
And they can join in with the dance of victory

Dare You?

Dare you walk by my side?
Dare you trust the One fit to be guide?
See the peace and liberty
In God's handiwork, for all to see

Can you walk in the forest glade
See the sunlight dapple in the shade
Nature rejoicing in His touch
And reach out for that which you've longed for,
so much

Can you dare to love the one
Who was there when time first began?
The one who felt the raindrops fall?
Heard the wind's first whispering call?

Can you hear the song that they sing?
Can you revel in the peace they bring
When worries drag you down
Can you wear a peaceful crown

Join the hymn that is life
With all it's worries and strife
It's still a beautiful place
This world and the space
We all live in and share

It is time to reach out and embrace
Nature, and our time and place
Protect the cradle that's borne me and you
And is born once more, anew, each spring

Dawn of Victory

Oh my child, listen to Me
Can't you see the agony?
Can't you see the blood I shed?
When I submitted the ground turned red

When I answered the costly yes
And rescued you from your distress
You had not even been born
Your eyes had never seen the morn

When I ended your captivity
I gave my life to set you free
Rejoice my child for I love you so
And in my love you will surely grow

The peace I have you surely seek
For I make you strong when you are weak
I work within your deepest soul
Mending your heart and making you whole

Yes, I loved you so I set you free
To give your heart in love for me
To serve the ones still torn with pain
To break the shackles, and to snap the chain

To walk the road with weary men
And teach them how to hope again
The hope that had been drowned in deep despair
To show them of a God who cares

So open that loving heart to me
And we will set the captives free
Showing them a brand new morn
A peaceful growing, loving dawn

Enthralling

Enthralling, Your love
Is calling me home

The boat comforts me
Yet, challenged by your love
I reach
The boat trembles, rocking
As I stretch

Frightened, I falter, I fall
And as I stumble
Once more I call

"Lord, save me!" I hear myself cry
Yet deep inside the lullaby You sing
Beckons me on, calling me home

And so I will reach
Knowing the beach
And our meal awaits
I will follow you
As You lead me

Home

Epiphany

On that first Epiphany
Those blessed Wise Men Three
Looking heavenward did see
A special star for you and me

On that cold and frosty night
That star that shone so bright
Dispelling darkness with its light
Spelt out to all so bright

That God saved Gentile and Jew
Christ came for me and you
No favours did He bestow
on the nations here below

The gifts those wise men brought
Many others have since sought
Gold, frankincense and myrrh
For our joy and despair

The babe in the manger, the stars in the sky
Tell to all people, salvation is nigh
The chains are now broken, your hands are now free
Tell all around you about your Epiphany

Evening Prayer

This day that has ended, Lord
Blessed though it be
Is never as wondrous
As those yet to be

And yes, we may falter
And yes, we may fall
His love will not alter
Nor cease his quiet call

So as we surrender
Our pain and fears release
To His love so tender
We receive His peace

Flowers Unchained

Look around and you will see
As you are walking next to me
All the joys and the fears
Walking in the path of tears

See the pattern of the rain
Bringing flowers forth again
In the deserts of their heart
See the love become a part

Of the dreams so long thought lost
When pain proved too high a cost
When the raging and the pain
Gave the fear its power again

Time to lock the fear and pain away
Walk from the night to day
Walk again in fields so bright
Dispelling again the deepest night

Look again and you will see
The love we have sets us free
When you're lost deep in your fear
Love will wipe away the tear

And once more we will see
The chains that once held us in
Are broken and we
Can once more begin

Reach out to prisoners once fellows of ours
And tell them that the powers
Of fear and pain have no hold
On the sons and daughters, we are told

Of a God whose love created the Earth
The heavens, the universe all given birth
By the One who stoops down from His throne
To once more give those who are His own
His love

Fury Untamed

I love you
You're my one true friend
My saviour and my friend
The one
Who turns my deepest night
To day
With the love that never ends

And when the fire
Burns with fury untamed
I cry
Call out your name
The steam cools
As your peace rules
In my heart

Raging,
Once more I look to you
And the life so painful
Once more
Opens the door
To you, and I am free

Don't ask me
How I know
But my love for you
Will always grow
For somewhere
Where I hide

This heart inside
You and I will know
Your peace

Glowing Embers

The fire glows, its embers sparking the night
Striking out with shards of light
Comfort, solace, all seem rare
In the darkness, the cold night air

The straggler wanders in alone
Bewildered, lost, looking to atone
The fire bringing welcome relief
Lets him express love and grief

Anger, pain, joy and despair
Hover in the midnight air
Love, deep, stronger than death
Is seen in another's breath

What is it I see in that other man's eyes?
That fear banishes and eases heartfelt sighs?
That soothes that anger, calms the pain
And lets me feel that healing rain?

When did the trust get broken
Where did it go?
Why did I stop reaching?
Will I ever know?

Was I ever meant to trust?
To reach out, I'm sure I must
Look at the scars, the wounded hand
Burnt by fires from many lands

Draw closer, stranger, watch the storm rage
My emotions doing battle on my broken heart's stage
When I perform, I put on quite a show
As that fire blazes, and the embers glow

If you look too close, you may well see
The ravaged soul that is really me
And out of that broken heart I peer
The windows of my soul are clear

I long for the friendship and love
Given by the Father above
The fire is a feeble spark
Sputtering in the world's spiritual dark

Look around, see the larger flame
Burning in praise of His Name
Walk out on the other path
Away from the spark and towards the fire
Let His love your heart inspire

Focus only on the love
You can see from God above
The journey is long, sometimes dark
And a long way from the comforting spark

But when at last, you reach that flame
And you utter praise to His Name
You'll reach the sunrise and the day
Lost in love so far away

Never more to see the night
Or wallow, broken in twilight
Lost in my Father's arms
Far from the Evil One's charms

Walk once more along the way
Listen to the words I say
Words of comfort, words of peace
That will once more give you release

Release to be who you really are
With no fear, no hold, no bar
Lose your fear and pain in Me
And we will set the lost ones free

God of Compassion

God of compassion, God of the weak
The blind man can see and the dumb can now speak
The lame man can walk and the lowly are kings
In the Kingdom of God, true justice He brings

God of the humble, God of all truth
God of the old man and God of the Youth
God of compassion, yes, Lord of all peace
Our hearts turn to you Lord and all conflict will cease

God of the anguished and God of the free
God of the night and the stars and the sea
God of the mountain and God of the plain
This Lord of compassion, with mercy shall reign

Swords, we need not, nor the halberd nor spear
All fall to the ground when the Saviour is near
The sun in the morning, the skies in the night
Waking and sleeping, Our God is our Light

Take our bitter fighting, take all our despair
And fill us with your peace, beyond all compare
Take hold of the hearts that are wounded by war
And fill our broken world with Your peace ever more

God of Our Salvation

Is the God of our salvation what you wanted
Him to be?
Do you see Him in the rich man, or in the
refugee?
Is His face pristine or dirty as He hangs upon
that tree?
Is the God of your salvation what you wanted Him to
be?

Do His arms reach out to everyone, not only to
the poor?
Do you hunger for His true peace, as you're
marching off to war?
Do the feet that were once pierced through
walk upon your battlefield?
Will you let His Spirit fill you, as to His love
you yield?

Do you listen to His whisper, and worry what
you'll hear?
Is the voice ever inspiring, blocked by a
deafened ear?
Is the gift of understanding burdened by an
unknown fear?
Do you see the war's true burden, and shed a
bitter tear?

Is the message that He carries, full of love that
is so true?
Simply meant for others, not really meant for you?
Does the message in the words you read, talk
deep within your soul?
Of a chance to stop the aching, and a chance to
become whole?

Stop the trying, stop the dying, learning simply
just to be
Ignore the world's demands, turn once again to Calvary
Block the clamour and the echo of our world
worn by its care
And see the true meanings of the words written there

It would be so easy to give up and fit in
To yield to the temptation, to fall back into sin
To climb back in the boat, far from the stormy sea
To turn your back upon the One who hangs
upon the tree

Or dare you risk the contact, dare you gaze into
His eyes
Would you gladly love the one the world has
chosen to despise?
Do you dare to risk the water, striding boldly
through the waves?
Grasping e'en more firmly the hand of the One
who saves?

Gather courage, gather strength, gather all that
you hold dear
Wage those battles once again, without that
bitter tear
Take the armour He will give you, the sword of
love and shield of peace
And fight upon another battlefield to win the
world's release.

Is the God of your salvation what you wanted
Him to be?
Is He locked up in your own heart, or have you
given Him the key
He can give all people in their lives the one true
liberty
If the God of your salvation is what He truly
wants to be ………

Your God

Headlong Into Your Arms

No matter the rage in the world outside
Your wounds proffer a place to hide
Away from the world so full of care
A chance to lose our deep despair

So easy to lose one's way
As the world speeds ahead each day
And as we come to each night
Thinking only of day's light

Stop once more, to be aware
We have an aching, deep, but there
The world is no answer to it's quest
Our soul and heart know what is best

Calvary's hill isn't popular now
We'd rather live crowded, and how
We shut the door on the child inside
The one who needs a place to hide

Let go, and once more let Him in
And the journey you'll begin
Where the world and it's lights will fade away
When we all see the true light of day

The light that comes from His face
Looking forward, with His grace
When in heaven we will be
With the One who sets us free

And lets the child once again
Be loved, instead of angry men
Berating anyone who's near
And doesn't know how to fear

But in the meantime, this I know
I have a safe place I can go
Once more unto that lonely tree
And in the wounds of the One who died
For me

Heartbeat of Peace

Deep in your heart, fear falls apart
The chains fall down, the thorny crown
Worn by thee now sets me free
Gives me liberty

Deep in your wounds, the heartbeat sounds
And in the womb of holy peace
I dream

The fire aflame blazes again
I hear your name and it enthralls me
Again

Once more I see
The one to set me free
And what I dare to be
Is what He gave to me?

Are these angry men?
Frightened once again
Their broken fear
Despite them being near
Condemns them to a life without you

If they only saw
Past their heart's closed door
Beggars, spiritually poor
They fear that more
May sweep their hearts away

Touch those hearts that fear
Lord, for thou art near
To the broken hearted
Frightened, weary guarded
Touch their angry heart
Let their healing start
Let your love be a part

Of their lives

Innocent Child

I, Your God sit back and cry
As once again the children die
For once again those bullets fly
And still their song

Do you know the touch of fear?
Can you see that silent tear?
When terror steals the childhood dear
And life is gone?

When the anger has all gone
Who is there to carry on?
When the bullets are all spent
Will the angry ones relent
To peace

Or will the war not be the last?
The lives are lost, they're dying fast
Is this the die that will be cast
To seal their fate?

Unload the rifle, cast it down
And unseat that evil crown
Look far beyond that rage, that fear
See once again that silent tear
That falls

Yes, turn that heart to one of peace
So once again gunfire will cease
And we will hear the children cry
No need for any more to die
Any more

So when the voice starts be raised
And eyes to rifles lift their gaze
Hear once again that children's song
And let the broken world belong
To Me

Just Surrender

Just surrender
My tender
Arms will enfold you
And I will hold you
Close to me, My child

For the world is so bitter
And twisted and torn
They throw you like litter
Out with the new morn

The waves are a-crashing
Pounding the land
Your heart they are smashing
Your life's in their hands

Angry they will take you
Smash your heart to bits
Leave you at the roadside
Wondering how it all fits

Just surrender, My tender
Love enfolds you, will hold you
Close to Me

And we can gaze the city's haze
Far from you and me
As we stand hand in hand
Beside Calvary

Rise as I, with the dawn
Joyfully we greet the morn
And no longer battered and torn
The pain that you have so long worn
Will disappear with the night
In the dawn of a new day

Kyrie Eleison

Kyrie eleison, my God please set us free
Christe eleison, on our misery
Kyrie eleison, wipe away each tear
Christe eleison, be ever near

Kyrie eleison, touch these hearts once more
Christe eleison, on each fruitless war
Kyrie eleison, heal our wounds so raw
Christe eleison, love us once more

Kyrie eleison, on the weapons we create
Thinking ourselves the master of our own fate
Christe eleison, as we wound each other
Causing pain to each sister and brother

Our hearts they turn to you, O Lord
Aching as we pay the price of the sword
"Enough of the pain" the people say
as we utter our heartfelt "Kyrie"

Labouring One

All you who labour come to me
And I will give you dignity
Lord loving Your humanity
Will set Your children free

Take the burdens that we bring
As we rejoice in you our King
Your kingship sets our hearts ablaze
To praise your name, Ancient of Days

Yes, take the pain that holds our fears
Release the anger and the tears
Dear Father let Your healing flow
Like a river, love us so

For we long so to be with You
Rejoicing in the things You do
Loving the way you set us free
Give us strength so we may be

Your child

Liberation Day

There are smiles on their faces
The first for many years
An end to the traces
Of countless heartfelt tears

As the lives were snuffed out
One by one, they all faltered
Lines of voices, did no-one shout?
As the country's profile altered?

Voices raised in angry protest
How quickly they disappeared
And the defections to the West
As for their lives the speakers feared

And as the holder of the terror
Bunkered down in his small cell
Felt for himself, in final error
The fear he used, often and well

For now the leader is a captive
And the repressed ones can go free
You can see them all rejoicing
In their new found liberty

But take a look into tomorrow
And gaze at what may lay ahead
Is it joy or is it sorrow?
For those living and those dead

We all should demand an answer
For those lost one's abandoned cries
And there should be an accounting
For crimes no one can disguise

So never again can one man rule
And threaten, terrorise, mutilate, maim
And command so much blind allegiance
At the mention of his name

For all mankind are born equal
We join and end the race the same
And why should we fear fellow racers?
Why should they be allowed to tame?

The one inside of every person
The children inside who are you and me?
How dare anyone imprison
A heart born into liberty?

And look again into the future
The beauty of a brave new morn
And into a liberated country
A new people is reborn

Life's Journey

Life is but a journey
And pilgrims on our way
We follow the Good Shepherd
He guides us through each day

The restful waters I can see
The mighty river flowing
His love provides the food I need
And my love keeps on growing

The fields beyond are full of peace
They promise us our shelter
The gate opens, and our release
From fire into the smelter

Lord, purify the hearts you made in us
Replace our hearts of stone
Our ills form when we turn away
Running from You alone

The fire that burns will clean our life
Cleanse with Your Holy flame
And amidst the toil and strife
We revel in Your Name

So, lead us by that peaceful stream
Guide us by that shore
And our broken hearts redeem
Both now and ever more

Light the Fire

Lord light the fire once again in the hearts of
angry men
Heal the wounds so sore evermore
So they may once more see
The everlasting beauty
To be found in peace

Light the fire of love in their heart
Maybe somehow they will start
With the spark that bursts into a flame
When they hear that voice
Have a choice
To hear and call your name

Take the raging and fill it with your peace
Take the longing, let the yearning cease

The fear of the love I cannot comprehend
It has no beginning has no end
And so I am lost
Deep in the fire of your peace
I find release
In the pain that won't cease
Till I let myself be totally set free
Unreservedly

Loose those chains once again
Embrace, Lord those angry men
So once again we may see
Lord, your love's beauty
Once more setting us free

Little Child

Little child within the manger
As we look back through the years
In the eyes of bygone strangers
We can see your unshed tears

As we kneel before your manger
Throne of heav'n left far behind
In the eyes of every stranger
Is the Lord of humankind

For as we join in adoration
With the oxen and the ass
We remember, once again Lord
How redemption came to pass

When with the tears of a newborn baby
Came the Lord of Life to men
And the message He brought to us
Taught us all to live again

As we hear the angel's chorus
Listen to that baby's cry
Heaven seems to be composing
An angel's glorious lullaby

While rejoicing in God's favour
In bestowing unto men
Their redeemer and their Saviour
The way to being born again

So remember in December
When the world is set up for war
And the battlefield is ready
What the baby's cry was for

As a herald of a new dawn
As a siren to the world
That in the new day, yes, the new morn
The King of Peace's banner was unfurled

And as we wallow in our feasting
As we simmer in our greed
Just remember, and consider
The oppressed who are in need

And for all who never see it
Let this Christmas be the first
Take the love of Christ our Saviour
To quench the hunger, ease the thirst

For the new life that he brought us
Life that is for ever free
Is enshrined in lessons taught us
As He hung on Calvary

And the triumph over suffering
His triumph over death
Brought to all the greatest gift
Love that conquered life's final breath

As we gaze upon that manger
And we think about that day
Let us look once more with wonder
At the child lain in the hay

Let us offer up thanksgiving
To the one who set us free
For the child within the manger
Is the Lord of life to me

Maybe Then...

There's trouble in the world Lord
We don't know what to do
Heartless ones attacking
Muslim, Christian, Gentile, Jew

They pound us with their values
They curse us with their pride
They wound us with their terror
And yet, we will abide

Our faith, it is in you Lord
In faith, hope and charity
We fear not Satan's wielded sword
We turn our face to thee

For we are all your children
Muslim, Christian, Gentile, Jew
We are fellow pilgrims
In our journey Lord, to you

While the war is now raging
We can see, Lord, as we fight
Spiritual battles we are staging
Against the darkness and the night

Change their hearts, these men of evil
Turn their souls to you anew
Teach them tolerance and mercy
Teach them Lord, to follow you

Maybe then we live as brothers
Maybe then we'll live in peace
Maybe then we'll love each other
And from terror be released

Mighty One

See Him, the Mighty one
He strides across mountains and seas
The rain calls
As it gently falls
Dancing patterns on the plain

And I will
Follow the one
Who wrote the song of my days
Praising, rejoicing once more
In the living God and his ways

For his ways are far above
The earth and all the bounty it holds
The harvest we shall reap
The rest that we shall sleep
He gave us for our own

Watch how the trees sway
Gently in the breeze
See Him rejoice in his child
As we gaze on our knees

For He knew we would stray
He knew when we would fall
He knew we wouldn't listen
To his constant call

His Son he sent to redeem
For he had a dream
When child and father came
And once more were the same

And when the wind bitter and cold
Bites my heart, makes me old
The aching I feel gets deep and is real

Will I then desert?
The path he has given to me?
Or will I gladly shoulder the cross
and walk once more to Calvary?

For the love I have inside
Is impossible to hide
When I feel the love I know is mine

And when I hear the song
I have to sing along
For the One who sets me free
Is living in me

Touch me, and heal me my Lord
And once more we dwell in unity
And this world torn
It's sorrow is born
As you hang on the tree

When you are raised
You are truly praised
For the chains around our heart are lost
And we gaze in awe
At the love you bore
And the pain borne at such a cost

Merciful Father

Merciful Father
Your love falls like rain
Blessed Redeemer,
it soothes all our pain

Lord the world is so broken
There's so much despair
The words that are spoken
Will show how you care

Can't you see that they're crying?
In the depths of the night
And the love of the father
Is burning so bright?

And yet they turn away
Afraid of the new day
Raging they falter
Hurting they fall
And heed not
The Father's call

Reach out to heal them
Reach out and show them
The world may be broken
And yet

He is there by their side
To love and to guide
Replacing fear and regret

With his peace

My God

My God, my King
We see
The pain the world feels
As I stand and gaze
Across the haze
Created by
Wounded men's tears

I see their swords
Their shields
Litter the field
As to their fears
With raging tears
And pain they yield

And yet they can't see
Blinded by their own pain
Tormented by the thirst
That you alone
Can satisfy

Laying their swords at your feet
Will render the journey complete
And healing begins
For when they see
And the healing they need
Maybe then we will be
Redeemed

See the field again
Without the tears of pain
And your love like rain
Will fall
Your love like rain will fall

Nowhere To Run

In the cold damp air
Fleeing takes me nowhere
For in the shadow of the gun
There's nowhere left to run

Man or woman, slave or free
Doesn't really matter to me
For when you're scared and on the run
There's still nowhere left to run

From the dread of the grave
God did His children save
For the slave man or the free
For the homeless refugee

Rich man, poor man, Gentile, Jew
There is a haven for you
A place where you can turn and hide
And heal those wounds so deep inside

In the depths of darkest night
Look closely you will see a light
Beyond the barrel of the gun
There is, at last, a place to run

And when at last you reach that shore
And those guns fire no more
You'll find your peace, your liberty
As you stand below Calvary's tree

Oasis

There are times
The barricades fall
And once again, we can give completely

When the rain
Touches the barren desert
Of a heart,
Joy slides like a smooth silk

Covering the brokenness
Soothing the emptiness
Filling the cracks, healing, accepting

Once more life so long forgotten
Reaches to the One who gives peace

The chains are smashed
The hearts in pain are released
Love purges all anguish
Peace flows, filling our brokenness
No condemnation we feel
For the love that frees us, redeems us

Sets us free, so we can be
Part of the rain soothing the pain
Healing the hurt, cleansing the dirt of anguish away

Bringing the light into deepest night
And the chance for them to stay
In the light of the day

A chance to live, a chance to forgive
An oasis of peace, a chance to release
And take our pain away

Old Armour

The more I keep falling
The more you keep calling my name

And the more I am raging
You keep on assuaging my pain

With the armour before
I felt so secure
Now uncertain I stand
My sword and shield in my hand

I am tired of the fight
I fought with all of my might
And now the night seems so near

The scarred landscape here
Echoes my scars I fear
Yet the familiar here bids me stay

So alone I am torn
Scared of both night and morn
With the armour I've worn all my days

It weighs me down
And I long for the crown
Of thorns instead, fixed upon my head

So weary I stand, in an unfriendly land
With my anger and fear unwanted sentinels here

And as I gaze in isolation
At Your own humiliation
The man upon the tree
Who felt once so like me

But He arose up from the grave
People like you and me to save
And God s greatest sign of victory
Is hung upon a tree

For through death He hath bought life
And a peace to end all strife
Rich and poor, gentile and Jew
All God s children born anew

And the armour I have worn
Is now battered, broken, torn
I lay them down at Calvary
To praise the One who set me free

Open Our Hearts - Pentecost

Open our hearts to Your Holy fire,
Open our hearts to it's flame
Your presence soothes our deepest desire
Our souls sing at the sound of your Name

Open our lives to the Spirit filled world
And give our souls their release,
As we stand on your mountains, our banners unfurled
Open our hearts to your peace

Open this world that's so tattered and torn
Pour forth from the river of love
Baptise us again, and we shall be reborn
In the fire of the Spirit above

The fire of that Spirit, aflame in our hearts
Setting all of our lives ablaze
Your Spirit infills us, and terror departs
Lost in our wondrous praise

The languages merge, our voices they blend
As one people united we sing
From baptism, beginning unto the end
Rejoice! In the Risen King

Look at the victory our Saviour has won
The price that was paid, at such cost
The Spirit He gave us, making us one
On the feast that we call Pentecost

Our Father

Our Father, where are you?
In the Gentile and the Jew
In the world that's torn in two
You see me, why can't I see you?

Our Father, God of peace
When will all this fighting cease?
When will the prisoner be free?
And the fears leave the refugee?

Yes, Our Father, God of love
Reach down from heav'n above
Touch the cold hearts made of stone
Make them long for you alone

Our Father, where are you?
I'm in the Gentile and the Jew
Lift your eyes and you will see
The end of your captivity

So reach out that hand, place it in mine
See in the bread and in the wine
The Risen God who saves you
Our Father, in the Gentile and the Jew

Pacesetting

The Lord is my pacesetter, so I am told
So why do I have times I feel weary and old?
If my actions and words are always in His sight
Then why can I wake in the deep of the night?

With a heart that is pounding, a mind full of fear
Searching in vain for the One who is near?
And no matter the things that I do or I say
Why does He always feel so far away?

I set aside places, I set aside time
And yet, life can feel like one crazy long mime
Not yet a reality, much less a fact
I wait for the curtain to finish the act

Somehow, without words, and without reason why
I find my one comfort, for by and by
As my heart rate slows down and my eyes close to sleep
I know that my God my soul will keep

Safe from all the bitterness and all the despair
That dwell in the ocean of life and it's lair
The monsters that dwell in the depths of life's see
No longer hold any terror for me

And though I may suffer at times from despair
And weariness deeper than most, I still dare
To reach out once more to Calvary's tree
And talk once again to the One, who for me

Gave His life and His love to all who would seek
The poor and ill-used, the mild and the meek
The gift that is given, to mild-mannered or proud
Is there for the quiet, as well as the loud

So when I awake in the dead of the night
I think of the One who put death to flight
And somehow the dread, with all it's fear
Is once more banished, and He again near

So, maybe I need simply be aware
Of His love ever faithful and His tender care
And know that wherever His servant may be
He will always listen and have time for me

And less important is when, where and how
For my God, is here, then, there and now
I can reach out, wherever and whenever I need
To satisfy hunger, and thirsting and feed

So, Lord, be my pacesetter, each moment, each day
And be thou my lantern that will light my way
So long as my journey is always with thee
My chains will drop lightly and once more I'll be free

Papa

Papa please hold me
Dear papa, enfold me

When the world's lights blind my eyes
When the words that are spoken drown my
anguished cries
Remember this broken child needs Your love

Wants to live as you desire
Has the flame sparking the fire
As your love sets me aflame
On fire with the sound of your name

This world tires, inspires
And the day is long
I can be strong only through your love

Sit with me under Calvary's tree
Set my heart free
And I will be at peace
In you

Peace Unbidden

Peace unbidden
All around I see
Mercy flows like a river
Floods both the world and me

Food for the hungry
A world for the meek
Voices for the broken
Healing I seek

Walk among the weary
Shed tears along the way
Heal the ones so wounded
Talk to me each day

I wish I could reach them
Tired and angry men
Show them you are the answer
And how to hope again

Believe in rainbows
Standing in the rain
Understand love once more
Whilst drowning in pain

Give joy a chance
Let My peace dance
Darkness will vanish
And fear we will banish

Peace unbidden
Yet in our lives He bids us dare
To the broken and the lonely
To show how He and you care

Pictures of Faith

Pastels colour the pages
Giving the shading,
Background to a life
Grounding to a world broken and alone

Details, shimmer into existence
Lovingly placed
The artist colours the heart
Of each child
Fashioned in perfect love
Held in the palm of His hand

When did the awareness fade?
How did the colours lose their freshness?

Lord, the world is jaded
War breaks the canvas
Spreading anger and pain
Thrusting rain, dark clouds
Threaten the peace

Reach down Lord
Soothe the fevered brow
Heal the raging ones
Soothe their anguish
Hold them in their pain

Let them know
That in the midst
Of clouds and rain
The rays of a sun on fire
With celestial light
Pierces through

Healing the broken
Curing the blind
Binding the shattered
In heart and in mind

Show them once more
As their chains release
That the love they abhor
Is the key to their peace

Show them the light
In the midst of despair
In the depths of the night
Shines a hope beyond compare

Anger will vanish, pain will ease
Just as the raging of the wind and seas
Ceased at Your call

For, my Lord
You can, and do, heal all

And so they cry in the depths of their fear
To reach they try
So far, yet so near

Teach them Lord
As they reach out to you
That to dare is to live
And to truly live
Is to love

In you

Rage and peace

No matter the rage in the world outside
Your wounds proffer a place to hide
Away from the world so full of care
A chance to lose our deep despair

So easy to lose one's way
As the world speeds ahead each day
And as we come to each night
Thinking only of day's light

Stop once more, to be aware
We have an aching, deep, but there
The world is no answer to it's quest
Our soul and heart know what is best

Calvary's hill isn't popular now
We'd rather live crowded, and how
We shut the door on the child inside
The one who needs a place to hide

Let go, and once more let Him in
And the journey you'll begin
Where the world and its lights will fade away
When we all see the true light of day

The light that comes from His face
Looking forward, with His grace
When in heaven we will be
With the One who sets us free

And lets the child once again
Be loved, instead of angry men
Berating anyone who's near
And doesn't know how to fear

But in the meantime, this I know
I have a safe place I can go
Once more unto that lonely tree
And in the wounds of the One who died
For me

Rain and Drought

Here he comes
Sitting at the well of my heart
Ready to drink of my experiences
And my pain
To soothe my barren desert
With drops of gentle rain

Do I stay?
Trapped by yesterday
And fearful of tomorrow?
The memories haunting me
Of loneliness and sorrow

The desert drains me
Taunts me, inspires me
To reach for water anew
And to taste that living water true

So as I see the one
Sitting by the well
I long to sit beside Him
My story to Him tell

Walking across I take a seat
He turns, I look, and our eyes meet
His eyes lock me in His gaze
And all I am, have ever been
Plays out in midday's haze

Drained, I fall down at His feet
His love will keep me safe
He wraps me in His loving arms
His child is once more safe

The water at the well is free
It flows deep for you and me
The One who sits there waits for us all
And in our hearts we hear His call

To drink

Raindance

Come and listen to the rain
Dancing on the window pane
Wave goodbye to every fear
As we wipe away each tear

Come and watch the rain once more
Patter gently on the door
Feel the freshness of the breeze
Learn again to be at ease

When the days just pass you by
In the blinking of an eye
It's so easy by and by
To sit and wonder why

Where did all those raindrops go
Why the mountains have the snow?
Where do people journey on
When their days on earth are done?

Take time to judge again
The priorities of men
Learn to heed our Father's call
Turn from life's hectic brawl

Take your life and be at peace
Let your inner strivings cease
Take a rest, and then again
Walk amongst those angry men

Teach them of a better way
Leading from dark to day
And maybe one day they'll see
The light will set their spirits free

Once more

Reach Out

Just reach out your heart to Me
I'll set your spirit free
To be all that you can be
If you just reach out to me

Just call out my Name
Forgetting any shame
Forgetting any fear
For I, the Lord, am near

Forget the pain that haunts
Forget those foolish taunts
Come, hide yourself in Me
As we hang upon this Tree

You know the voice inside is Me
You know that love is victory
My love is your destiny
Come child, share eternity, with me

Redemption

The servant King wears a crown
And our sins they all drown
Washed away, washed down
By the blood of the Lamb
As it flows ever on

The sheep all rejoice
At the true shepherd's voice
And the hearts of his people
Rejoice once again

In His love
This river endlessly flowing
To the God of all-knowing

The true victory
Shown in Calvary
Once more is complete
As death sits at His feet

The One who washed the feet of men
Is risen once again
Through the death on the cross
The ultimate loss
Sin is defeated
It's hold ne'er repeated

Let us feel no shame
In the sound of your name
Let us do your will
Your love guide us still

The power of your voice
The love gives us choice
To serve broken men
To live once again

Break the chains of the fears
Stop our pain, ease our tears
As we cry through the years
For our own release

And through these bitter wars
Which all have one cause
Service to our fellow men
Help us to enact once again

For to serve one another
And to call each man brother
You prayed for that day
When your death did say
Victory

Teach us to serve each other
Each sister and brother
Giving dignity
As we set them all free

And follow your lead
Help them in their need

And light forth the way
In this world of today
For when we are called
To leave this place
We know we will find
a loving embrace

From the one who was servant
And now is the King
As He sits on the Throne
The hosannas ring

As we lay down our crowns
In worship and praise
At the feet of that servant
The Ancient of Days

Remembrance

The leaf spirals downwards
blown by the breeze

The poppy bends, swaying in the fields
as the wind caresses it's stalk

Voices unbidden, echo hauntingly through the grass
of young men long since dead, upon this grassy plain

Can you hear it? Their Last Post?
Mournfully recalling the waste
What a cost

With rifle and helmet they sat
Knee deep in trenches
Losing faith as they lost their limbs
in a waiting game with no winners

Stand for a minute or two
and reflect on their sacrifice
you and I are free
as those men, barely adult
paid our ransom

Yes, those who will not weary
or the years condemn
as we stand in mute thanksgiving
we will remember them

Rest

Rest in my loving arms my child
Rest in the peace that I can give
Rest, your heart meek and mild
Wounded, will have a chance to live

Rest once again, give your heart to me
Rest for my love will set you free
Strength I will truly give
As once more you will live
Rest, for the day is very near

Rest, for the day is close at hand
And we will we bring peace to this land
To this land
Broken the world may me
Battered, you are now free
Show my love freely giv'n to all

See how the world is bruised and hurt
Feel as we're buried in the dirt
Anger, rage, and despair
Lost in the rain we dare
Hope for the sunshine of His peace
Give this world a chance to be released

Rivers and Greed

They say a mighty river
Flowed along here
That the Lord, our life giver
Gave us to sustain our lives

Looking down at the dirty valley
Water left here long ago
We listen, eyes wide with wonder
When our elders talk of snow

Long ago, it seems water fell down
In rivers from the sky
And the water was forthcoming
So how did our world get so dry?

People overreached their needs, son
People overreached their world
And now their very greed, son
Has taken our lives

For we know not when it rains now
If water will fall from the sky
And without that precious liquid
We are all doomed to die

If only they had seen it
If only they had known
That the more that they overreached themselves
The more our doom was sown

Yes, the more that their greed
Outstripped their own need
The more they took away
From what we have today

As I look along the river
And close my eyes to dream
Instead of dusty banks now
I see a gushing stream

If only they had seen Lord
The mess that they were in
We wouldn't now be dying
Our lives are struggling

Is this to be their future?
Are we really to blame?
Do we want to leave this legacy?
Our generation shamed?

For we all can make a difference
We all can give and take
And if we learn to do so
We can a difference make

For the world is not infinite
Resources are so few
And without a chance to rest
The world will not renew

The dreamer of the future
May not have to dream
To see a mighty river
Or a gushing mountain stream

The choice is ours to make, friends
In our hands, yours and mine
Let's all make a difference
And give the future times
A chance

Saviour in the Mirror

I sometimes wonder, what does He see?
When my saviour looks at me?
Does He see the scars deep inside my soul?
Or just a chance to make the broken one whole?

Does He see the burdens or just the smile?
Does He know I take the extra mile?
Does He see the stumbling steps I take?
Or the beauty of the heart that breaks

The times I feel right, you're by my side
You show me a beauty right deep inside
There's a beautiful person, a precious seam
The child He chose to love and redeem

So when I feel ugly and worthless and old
I ignore the world with its temptations so cold
I look for the beauty so deep inside me
And thank the Lord above for making me…

Me

Scars of Beauty

Beauty unspoken
Peace unbroken
Mirror suddenly shattered
Shards all that mattered

With one act
Broken is the pact
Years of pain begin
With the arrival of sin

Beauty marred
Broken, scarred
Feet, hands, head and side
The Son of God, crucified

Blood flowing, endless, free
Bathe us in Your victory
Death and sin no more to win
A new life we can begin

Bridging that mighty divide
Seated at the Father's side
Between Father, Spirit and the Son
The battle over, love has won

Beauty now unbroken
Words of love now spoken
Bread and wine we've shared
Listened to His word

Praise the One who gave His life
To end for good, anguish and strife
Who spoke those words on Calvary
And died to set humankind free.

Selfish Steward

Hovering, the waters rage
The Spirit lingers
The seething ceases, it is time

The touch of the Father's hand
And the first land rises
Majestically
The waves part, as the new land is born

Plants fill the earth
Bringing to birth life, and the cycle
That will bring forth creatures
And man

Nature in harmony, the earth rejoices
The water chuckles, and, raising their voices,
The creatures adore their gentle Maker

Man appears
In God's own image
The steward of a world
Teeming with life
All was good, God rested

Man, selfish and stubborn
Subdues the earth
And the birth of greed is complete
The once complete cycle is broken
Words that are spoken by nature's heart

Now speak of pain,
As that which remains is plundered
Without respite, without thought

And yet, we do not just rifle through a finite box
Scrabbling to waste what we can

Our fellow man dies, his cries unheard
As we scrabble to have more of the earth's treasure
Unequal measure condemns our fellow creatures
And humanity itself to a hungry grave

It's time, take your head from the box
Listen to the cries
And take heed of the wise

The Spirit will heal our wounded ways
And our days will fill with peace
When we release our selfish hands
And lay them free to rediscover
Humanity

Shalom

Shalom my friend, shalom
My peace to you, shalom
As I look down the barrel of your gun
I wish you shalom

I give to you my peace
Don't let your finger release
The death that's in your hand
My blood will stain your land
With my shalom

I leave with you my joy
Your gun cannot destroy
The gift I have to share
The joy beyond compare
In my shalom

Shalom my friend, shalom
Put down that trusty gun
Reach out your hand to me
And one day you'll be free
To give your shalom....

To me

Sometimes

Sometimes the road seems long
And I don't seem as strong
As when I first began

On these days my heart pays
Attention to those flights
And deep in those nights
My soul loses it's way

For as the night holds sway
And the dawn is hours away
My mind drifts, my heart shifts
And all too soon the currents
Sweep me away

To a distant land where another's hand
Guides me in forests deep
In the midst of sleep
And so I am swept away

And as the night bids a fond farewell
I am abandoned for a spell
To the depths of unhastened sleep
Where unshed tears have a chance to weep

Again I see a waterfall, and once more hear Him call
Stretching forth His hands to me
Bidding me to liberty

My armour strong, now weighs me down
If I wade in, I'll surely drown
The buckles and the weapon true
No longer help my journey through

So I am lost with armour held
With shackles of my fear they meld
My stubborn feet to the floor
And lost I hear my spirit roar

I drop the armour, to be free
And try to grasp my liberty
But fear and rage hold me again
Afraid of bitter, angry men

So torn, I let my spirit be
And try to give myself to He
Who long ago on a lonely hill
Give His life, my fears to still

For although still lost I stand
I know I've found my promised land
And at last I'm truly free
To celebrate your victory

Space

There are times I need space
In my heart, there's a place
I have to keep just for me
To hold my sanity intact

A lesson hard to learn
When I had to turn
And walk right away
Because to stay
Would lose my way
Never to return

And oft tho I yearn
To give and to learn
Once more how to trust
For my own good, I must
Back away

I have given too much
Of myself, this past year
And out of touch
With myself, I fear
I no longer can say who I am

So I stay out of reach
Needing once more that beach
The solitude of nature
That touches the child in me

Don't take offence, it isn't pretence
I no longer know who I am, where to go
Who to love, and to trust
So for all friends I must disappear

And maybe one day
These fears far away
I can once more believe
In the child, who'll retrieve
The love that I placed
In that barren waste
I call my heart

So please don't take offence
And let commonsense
See the battles I fight
With my own fear and fright
Rage on both day and night
And the armies I face
With God's powerful grace
Will be overcome

But as the battle is raging
It's time for engaging
The chance to get away
In those hills and pray
For some guidance

I never imagined
There'd come a day
When I wish for the silence
To beckon my way
And have on my mind
To go and pray

In a place of quietness
Where my father and I
Will listen once more
To the Spirit's lullaby

And as lay I rocking
Maybe then I will see
The price of forgiveness
On Calvary's tree

And sit far above battles
And wounds of the heart
So that once more
This child will start
To live

For now I see battles
Where maybe there's none
And I long for a victory
Through Christ, God's son

But maybe the battle
Is already fought
And all of the victories
With His blood He bought

So let me gaze briefly
On the barren, scarred soil
Where my heart in it's anguish
In battle did toil
And give me the strength, Lord
To face a new day
By taking armour and sword
And walking away

To peace

Spirit A-Sighing

I gaze alone, across the years
Seeing so much sorrow, and many fears
With no release for many tears
My spirit cries

And as I see, once again
The curled lips of the angry men
Words thrown both by mouth and pen
My spirit sighs

As the Gospel words are used
And the message is abused
By violent ones, whose laughter crude
Leaves my spirit crying

Take the message I am bringing
From the One who, angels singing
Praise eternally on His throne
And for those cruel words atone
For His Spirit is trying

To heal the wounds with words of peace
To once more make the fighting cease
To ease the heart of every fear
And wipe away every tear
And ease the sighing

For as He watches broken child
The one who was so meek and mild
His heart, so open to us all
Is once more making His strong call
And His Spirit trying

To heal the hatred once again
And touch the wounded hearts of men
And watch at peace once again
The Spirit of God's peace flying
Free

Spirit of Peace

Bringer of peace
All strivings cease
Life in peaceful harmony
Set by Your Spirit, free

The battlefields are silent now
The earth swallows cries
Of innocents slaughtered
As violence denied them goodbyes

Reach out, God's children all
Weapons dropped, hear His call
Father, set our hearts free
Give us the liberty

The world promises
Yet cannot deliver
As once more we discover
There is only one giver

Father, hear our anguished cries
Hear the wounded one's sighs
Give us compassion anew
So we can turn the broken world to you

And peace

Starry Night

Starry night, gently keeping
guard over a world that is sleeping
Makes me feel the restful way
That life prepares for the next day

Majesty of a God of Love
Echoed in the stars above
If you're lucky, you'll see Mars
Or Venus playing with the stars

Yes, the night makes me feel small
the view of stars leaves me enthralled
Thinking how lucky I must be
For the God that made them, He loves me!

Stormy Waters

The waters rage
My soul, troubled, seeks solace
In their savagery

Here He comes
I see Him, His feet
Gliding across the water

I reach out, longing for the peace
He offers

The storm once more arises
My frightened heart rears nervously

Peace, be still
Take courage, I am with you

Slowly, the waves settle
The wind drops,
And I am at peace
With You

Surrounded

Surrounded, astounded
I gaze at the gifts
You give to man

And yet we fail to see
All around, humanity

Is killing beauty, savages, we hack
Desecrating the work Your hands have made

How can you bear it?
I can see the pain wreaked
By angry children

Lost and afraid, they rage
Destroying all in their path, their wrath
Uncontrollable
Their pain inconsolable

Except for the One they will not see
Who sets them free?
He holds the key

The one who crafted the world
Who laid fast the land?
And with a thought
Outstretched His mighty hand

Painted the sunsets
Living, vivid, passionate, free
And yet loved enough
To set His children free

Can you imagine?
What pain he must bear
As His errant children
Rage in despair

So I will weep
For the ones lost
And vigil keep
With the one who paid the cost

Of love

Take the Time

O my people, listen to the words I have to I say
Open up your hearts, don't turn your backs and walk away
Listen to the words I give in their entirety
The truth in all its wholeness will set your spirit free

Don't take my words and mould them, interpreting what you feel I have to say
Don't listen to the parts you like and simply walk away
The light of the new dawn is merely precursor to the day
Would you, yourselves, be satisfied with knowing half the way?

Still your minds and still your hearts, my children, every one
We all know of the work ahead, the task that's to be done
There's time enough for planning when the work will start
I need you now to listen and to open up your heart

Open up that heart of yours and hear the anguished cries
The pain of those wounded ones, their struggles and their sighs

Unblock those deafened ears and unloose those blinkered eyes
Allow yourselves to do my work, see my Love in their eyes

Open up that heart of yours, to let my love flow through
Let my heart beat in time with yours, there's so much left to do
This weary world is tired and old, it's time to make anew
And fill it with my Spirit, ever ancient, ever true

So take the time to listen, take the time to share
Take the time to show the God you worship is still there
Take the time to still your soul, take the time to be
And deep within that restless heart, you'll find one day, you're free.

Teetering Temptation

Teetering
As the darkness beckons me
I linger
Looking down
The old ways haunt me
Taunt me, enticing me
To lose who I am in who I was

I close my eyes
Raising my head
I see the other path
Not easy, not simple

The road is broken
Shattered
The surface is broken
Yet I know
Your rod in my hand
Bids me leave
My life
In Your hands

Those hands
Pierced for my sins
Such love
Incomprehensible
In it's enormity
Enfolds me
And holds me
As I rest
In You

Hope restored
Your love outpoured
To broken men
We once again
Will reach

Tossed Leaves

The sound of the trees
As their leaves in the breeze
Are caressed with the slightest touch

Speaks once again of the folly of men
Lost in their own way to the light of the day
That is dawning

So I watch and wait as their fate
Is blown like the leaves
On the tree

And as I watch, they try to scotch
The rumours that maybe
They are as helpless to Thee
As those leaves on the tree

And I marvel still
That Thou will
Reach out Your hands to me
The leaf on that tree

And keep me sheltered
From the storm
That blows outside
I am warm

Safe in the arms
Of the One
Who to rescue me
Sent His Son to die

For the ones on the tree
Who are now free
Blown we may be
Tossed, broken and torn
By this world so careworn

And yet we find peace
From the storm's violent heart
And a deep release
Once we've played our part

So I rest content
Knowing when my life is spent
I will lie in your harms
Far from the world's charms

And that gives me strength
To last through the length
Of the time I am here
For I know you are near

And when my time comes
As it will come to all
I will not fear
When it's my time to fall

For the end of the fall
Is to land in Your heart
The one who created me
For I am a child of God

And I rest in peace
in you.

The Barriers

Take down the barriers
Knock down the wall
Come down from your fortresses
Heed my gentle call

Your isolation protects you
Yet tears at your heart
While you take shelter
Lonely child, torn apart

By the walls that surround you
Dear child, you're hemmed in
Come out of the fortress
A new life begin

For you, alone, my child
To the door have the key
Dig deep in your heart's pockets
And open your soul
To me

The Carpenter's Son

I surrender all
And helplessly fall
As I hear You call
Out to me

I once more embrace
That wounded face
That man who set me free
The man from Galilee

The carpenter's lowly son
The longed for Holy One
The Blessed Son of God
My feet in His steps have trod

Open the heart that has felt such pain
Open my heart Lord to let You reign
Teach me to love You, to let go of my pride
Come into the secret room where I hide

When the world batters like a raging storm
Let my Love for You help me to be reborn
And when the fear and rage subsides
Let me be the one who hides…

Deep in You

The Cloister

Shadows line the cloister wall,
I feel the summons, hear the call
No sound echoes in this holy place,
No praises of God's Holy Grace

Yet the call I feel is God's, I know,
Where my feet lead, I will go
For I see a vision not of my sight,
A vision of my God tonight

A figure sat in robes so coarse,
I feel the pain, the man the source
I turn away, for it pains me so,
And yet I cannot leave, I cannot go

My heart fumbles, my mouth inept,
As I see the sight I can't accept
The figure in cloth in so much distress,
I sense is our Saviour, I can say no less

The pain I feel is His, I'm sure,
The world cannot offer Him a cure
No secular thing can succour relief,
For this kind of passion, this type of grief

Give us the strength to heal Your pain,
Show us the way to let You reign
In a world that is bitter, so full of despair,
In a world full of cowards, let us dare......
To love You

The Kingdom of the Poor

Here in this place where the love is freely given
Where rich and poor are now seated at the feast
   There is no distinction, no rank or position
   For at the table sit the greatest and the least

   Here at this banquet love is overflowing
   Where peace and justice walk hand in hand
   Here in this broken world our knowing
     Of God's love will heal our land

When all the nations will their bitter conflicts
When all the wars and the bitterness will cease
When man and woman from every nation
   Join together to search for true peace

When all our searching has led the whole globe over
When all our wisdom has stretched to no avail
And our hearts still yearn for that belonging
It's time to follow that well trodden trail

   It wanders through the noisy city
   Through the hedges and the fields
   Through the bustle of our own lives
     Until to the Spirit we yield

   For at the end of the restless journey
   When we've reached the final goal
   No matter our faith, no matter our road
     Our lives can never be whole

Turn to the one who hung on the cross
For life's victory was His loss
Thorns crowning a Sacred Head
Risen once more from the dead

Look no more at the world for the cure
Look once again as often before
At the one who submitted to the grave
Whose victory alone has power to save

Turn away from the bustle of our life
Turn from our battles and our strife
Golgotha's hill, full of peace
Will our bound hearts release

Yes, turn to that man, and be reborn
Face the glorious new morn
Tell all those around, all those you see
Of the price He paid to set us free

The Leaf

The leaf ,holds firmly to the branch of life
Knowing that the tree will sustain

The little springtime
So precious with sunshine
Piercing with golden rays
Peeks shyly through the glade
And the leaf exalts in its warmth

Safely, it hangs
In the safety of the tree
Sustaining it, giving it life and true peace

Storms rage, yet the leaf
Clings fearlessly
Knowing it is secure

The wind
Caresses the leaf
Teases it, easing gently
The stem from it's resting place

The leaf is carried
And comes to rest in peace

He placed his hand
In your wounded side
Now Lord, he is at peace
Knowing he can truly hide
In You

R.I.P Frere Roger, Taize

The Sacred Lonely Olive Tree

Seated under the darkness, sheltered neath the olive tree
The only people here tonight, the Father and Me
The people I chose as friends, all raced away
I dread the approach of the coming day

The dawn seems so near, and yet tonight
I know the dawn is far too bright
In the near future I can see
the cross they have prepared for Me

Tell me, tell me Father so dear
When My death is so close, so near
Why does the path not seem so clear?

When we started it was so new
This love we have, Me and You
Can I give this chalice back
Can I just turn away, show the world my back?

Surely you can save them without my death?
Do I have to draw my last breath?
Do I have to give my Life away
to allow them to see a new day?

Oh, Father, do what you must
This is no time for me to be losing my trust
This cross you have in store for me
Is to be a sign of your greatest victory

The crown of thorns, the bloodied head, the wounded side
The last words that I cried
"It is finished, " the words I scream to thee
The task you have given to Me
I have set Your children free

The Shelter

There Lord, I see them
The thorny crowns, the pierced side
The scars bid me welcome
And in your love I hide

Deep in your wounds Lord
Hide and comfort me
You are my true reward
Cup of life to me

When storms rage
Outside, in my heart
I am on that stage
Playing my part

Shattered, and broken
I stagger away
Wounded, exhausted
The act in the play

We call life
Has once more drained me
It's constant strife
Will not let me be

Ensnared, I reach
Trapped by rage, I fall
Tumbling, faltering
Frightened, once more I call

Bewildered,
my voice cries to thee
Knowing You alone
can set me free

It seems so crazy
That there should be
Warrior and peacemaker
Living inside of me

And when the soldier
Weary of the fight
Lays down armour
And sleeps till light

The peace they seek
Will not be found
In blood stained battles
Pain all around

So I will reach
And once more return
Where the fires
In my heart do burn
And once again
I will turn

To the one I know
With pierced side
Thorny crown and wounded hands
And the shelter that they provide

For once more
I will rest
counting myself
Greatly blessed

Thorns of Pain

Prince of Peace, your heart is crowned
With thorns of pain, as angels surround
The wounds so grievous, they pierce you through
Let our service Lord be true

King of joy, we thee adore
Let us learn to love you more
As we sing the tune of victory
Show once more the wounds that set us free

As you hung between each thief
Your agony brought relief
To a world, thought wounded beyond repair
Giving it a chance to once more care

For the man carrying burdens way too hard
For the one being dealt life's losing card
For the slave, the wounded, the ones lost
They all praise You for paying the cost

The debt paid as you up the hill trod
The Holy one, the Son of God
The mighty one, come down to save
And rob death's power over the grave

The scars you wear, not ones to hide
We display them in our hearts
We can turn Satan's tide
By each one playing their parts

Let us praise the wounded King
Let us worship at His feet
For by His death and resurrection
His victory o'er death is complete

Throne of Grace

Walking in the Spirit's peace
I feel my aching soul release
All the strain it feels inside
And the tears it tries to hide

All the strain it tries to quell
As on the pain I try not to dwell
And look around, for what I seek
A chance to listen, a chance to speak

And as I journey through the land
Offering Christ's outstretched hand
The masks they wear fit oh so well
And condemn them all to living hell

For as the Spirit moves me on
I wonder where compassion's gone
I wonder who can ease their plight?
And waken their heart's deepest night

Who can heal their deepest wounds?
Who can soothe their deepest pain?
Who will listen as it sounds?
In the soul, echoes of falling rain

As they weary take their grief
Bound with a lack of relief
And trudge along the road of life
Ensnared by their trouble and strife

Look once again at the open road
Sit down my friend, and leave the load
Stretch out those hands, empty once more
And reach to peace, forever more

For as you reach you will find
The Son of Man who saved mankind
Is reaching down His hand to You
Hold on firm, He'll pull you through

For the life that we all live here
For all it's worry, woes and tears
Is but a stop along the way
Unto the place we'll reach someday

And leave the load that ties you down
You'll exchange it for a crown
When we arrive at that place
And bow in front of the Throne of Grace

Travelling Home

There are ways that we travel
Roads of the heart long and slow
There are times when the sunlight blinds me
And all that I know

Is we go there together
Our love and the peace keep me still
Knowing that in the deepest night
You are my sight, I love you still

When the road seems so long
No longer strong I turn to you
When the strength of the pain
Turns into rain
The skies above turn blue

For with you by my side
To lead and to guide
The rainstorm soaks me
Drenched, I am set free

My heart turns once more to you
To feel that love so true
To turn my love away
Would truly wound you

So wounded I stand
Old armour in my hand
Dropping sword by side
I wait for you to guide

Me home

Under the Tree

Look under the tree
Find the refugee
The rich and the poor
Slaves to pain no more

Look into its shade
It's canopy vast
No difference is made
Between first and last

The gift that is found there
Is priceless, yet free
And all can afford it
It's for you, and for me

Reach out to the broken
Reach out if you dare
The words that are spoken
Can show that you care

And if you are saying
My words will not do
Then by simply praying
I'll say them, for you

Children of God,
Black, white, rich, poor
Of many races
Languages and more

Yet we are all one
Sitting under that tree
And the gift that is given
For you and for me

Has no condition
Has no attached string
For freely is it given
By Saviour and King

And when we are burdened
As oft we can be
The load can be shed
Under Calvary's tree

Waves of Love

Walk along an empty beach
Feel the troubles flow out of reach
In the waves gentle swell
Is the Father's love we know so well

As we hustle and hurry our way through our life
As we scurry and scuttle, through troubles and strife
The city, so noisy, so soulless, so cold
Robs us of our lives, leaves us feeling so old

When we look to our future, tell me, what do we see?
Is it office block, skyscraper, computer or tree?
Do we truly remember the place we belong
Where the loudest disturbance is eager birdsong

Where the peace of the forest holds life in its way
Where the solitary night blends into day
Where the world is at peace, where our troubles cease
The city's life so far away

Do we realise the hunger, and hear our soul's cry?
To away from the city, to the sea and the sky
Where the cliffs and the water show us love within reach
God's love and His presence, shown best on the beach.

When You Listen

When you listen do you hear
The voice that is so near?
Watch the lantern, see the light
That dispels the deepest night
If you follow you'll find the way
From the night into the day

Do you revel in the rain
Without overwhelming pain
Do you give your feelings voice
And your heart time to rejoice

Do you find the time, and seek the key
To truly once more be set free
For the laughter of the child
Is the love of God so mild

Use your eyes and you will see
There is love and liberty
Use your heart and soul again
Join the song of peaceful men

Hear the chorus of the song
Of the ones we know belong
To the choir of the ones
He called to know they belong

So open your ears and open your heart
And together once more we'll start
To love the ones despised by men
And teach them all once again

To sing

Wolves of the Heart

Here they come those wolves
Paws pounding at the door to my heart
Swiftly they pace, stealth in human form
To pounce, ripping my heart to shreds
Smiling as they do so

They have no idea how it feels
To cower behind the walls
That we build to protect ourselves
Terrified one day
The wall will crumble
The mask will tumble
And we will be exposed

So, the wolves are here again
Almost forgotten, their presence taunts me
And I remember all too well
Their actions and the anguish I felt
The last time I smelt their scent in my heart

Tell me, that these wolves are not real
That they're really friendly dogs
And my imagination is playing tricks on me

Tell me, I am safe and secure
For once more I see the wolves
Beckoning at my heart's door

For now I can see that the one who protects me
From their fangs is the one who I welcome
Into my heart without reservation, yet not without trepidation
But with a deep sense of yearning
For peace I know He alone can give

Yearning

This yearning
Is turning
My head

This burning
And yearning
Proves I
Am not dead

These words
I am writing
Emotions
I'm fighting
And yet so exciting
Those tears that
I shed

The battles are raging
Then wars they are staging
But somewhere inside me
There's peace instead

A way of redeeming
And silencing screaming
The words that are scheming
One day to be said

120 Seconds

Leaves falling gently twirl softly
Dancing gracefully to the earth below

And as the leaves twirl slowly downward
To reach the soft earth below
It touches a grave of a soldier
Unmarked, unknown from long ago

For the meadow is silent now
Once again, a far cry
From the screams of wounded men dying

Later in the year these fields turn red
Remembering the fear and the dread

Bullets flying, many dying
Brave, victorious
Scared as hell
Was it still a battle glorious?
Hear the words survivors tell

Freedom, such a precious gift
Assumed by many as a right
Many fought, to seal that rift
Against the evils of the night

So take the time, our precious time
And let the silence steal but two
Precious minutes, such precious minutes
And remember them anew

For on the field, strewn red with poppies
Flanders, and so many more
The blood of young men flowed like rivers
So we may all be free once more

Do this I ask, yes please remember
Be it cold or be it wet
As we stand this day in November
We do all have to remember
Lest in our haste we forget

For if not for those poppy strewn fields
Our freedom would never have been
And all the people, different and unique
Would never have a new dawn seen

So, stand in silence and grateful silence
And give thanks for the price they gave
And mark you well 120 seconds
For the soldier's unmarked grave

The wind blows boldly through the treetops
Leaves swirl madly to the ground
And once again, that unmarked soldier
By the Father' loving touch is found.

And as I lift my gaze up from that meadow
As the leaves swirl madly by
If I listen, oh so closely
I can hear that mournful cry

For those 120 seconds
Look back at that great sacrifice
And think again with grateful love
About the ones who paid the price

For with their blood was freedom bought
They paid with tears, and blood and pain
And all that cost would be for naught
If we forget, those who remain.

www.ingramcontent.com/pod-product-compliance
Lightning Source LLC
Chambersburg PA
CBHW061649040426
42446CB00010B/1649